Wake Up to the World of Science

SMALL ANIMALS IN CAPTIVITY

B. Bornancin

Burke Books **▶**B *LONDON ∗ TORONTO ∗ NEW YORK*

First published in the English language 1983
Revised and reprinted 1984
© Burke Publishing Company Limited 1983
Translated and adapted from *Les animaux bien installés: Collection Bornancin-Mérigot*
© Editions Fernand Nathan 1981

Acknowledgements
The publishers are grateful to G. Lovett for preparing the text of this edition, and to the following for permission to reproduce copyright illustrations:
    Atlas-Photo, Bornancin, Jacana, Labat, Pitch, Tarlier. *Cover:* Six.

CIP data
Small animals in captivity. – (Wake up to the world of science)
    1.   Animal ecology
    I. Bornancin, B.   II. Mérigot, M.
    III. Les animaux bien installes. *English*   IV. Series
    591.52   QH541.14
    ISBN 0 222 00873 3
    ISBN 0 222 00874 1 Pbk.

Burke Publishing Company Limited
Pegasus House, 116-120 Golden Lane, London EC1Y 0TL, England.
Burke Publishing (Canada) Limited
Registered Office: 20 Queen Street West, Suite 3000, Box 30, Toronto, Canada M5H 1V5.
Burke Publishing Company Inc.
Registered Office: 333 State Street, PO Box 1740, Bridgeport, Connecticut 06601, U.S.A.
Filmset in "Monophoto" Souvenir by Green Gates Studios Ltd., Hull, England.
Printed in the Netherlands by Deltaprint Holland.

CONTENTS

RECORD CARD

NAME OF ANIMAL . . . .

DATE CAUGHT . . . .

DATE BORN (if known) . . . .

PLACE . . . .

SPECIAL CARE OF CAGE . . . .

FOOD . . . .

WATER . . . .

CLEANING. . . . .

Care and food vary according to the animals. If you caught them:
– in a meadow, see pages 13–21;
– in a humid place or in the forest, see pages 22–25;
– in fresh water, see page 26.

If you need more specific advice, consult the index.

4

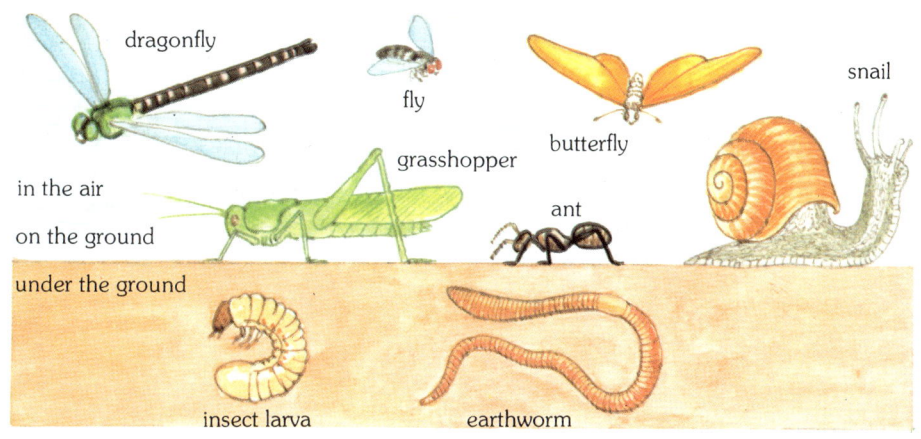

dragonfly

fly

butterfly

snail

grasshopper

in the air

ant

on the ground

under the ground

insect larva

earthworm

STUDY CARD

Where does it live? (its environment) . . . .

How does it live? (its functions) . . . .

- **Food**
  What is its food? . . . .
  Does it prefer certain types of food? . . . .
  How does it eat the food? . . . .
  Does it dispose of waste products? . . . .

- **Breathing**
  What organs are used? . . . .
  Where are they found? . . . .

- **Movement**
  How? . . . .
  With what organs? . . . .
  When? . . . .
  Why? . . . .

- **Senses**
  Can it see? . . . .
  Can it hear? . . . .
  Can it feel? . . . .
  How does it react? . . . .

- **Reproduction**
  Is it male or female? . . . .
  Will it lay eggs? . . . .
  Establish its life-cycle . . . .

What animals eat it? . . . .
Draw up a food chain . . . .

Very simple cages

You can obtain an ordinary aquarium which you can cover with fine mesh wire. Or else you can make a cage.

Watching small animals helps you to understand them and their role in nature. To do this, you have first to capture them and then to keep them – for as short a time as possible – in conditions similar to those of their natural habitat. Once your observations are complete, you should return the animals to the place where you found them. Whilst they are in your care, you should be patient and attentive – you will be amazed at what you discover.

A green frog on a leaf. Note the adhesive pads at the ends of its toes

If you are even more ambitious you can make a cage like this.

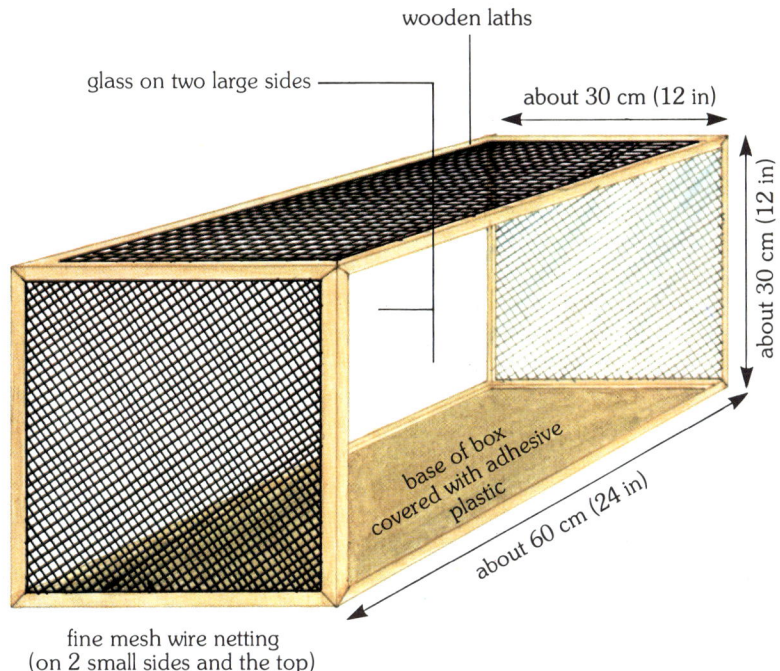

wooden laths

glass on two large sides

about 30 cm (12 in)

about 30 cm (12 in)

base of box covered with adhesive plastic

about 60 cm (24 in)

fine mesh wire netting
(on 2 small sides and the top)

This type of cage will be suitable for all types of animals. The interior will have to be arranged to suit the life of the animal you are studying. You should always try to imitate the environment of the captive animal.

You can observe insects, spiders, scorpions, grass-snakes, lizards, slow-worms, etc.

"With a few pebbles, a little sand, a little greenery and some tasty mealworms, captivity will be quite pleasant."

Catching equipment

1. Useful everyday equipment

All those boxes, containers and empty jars which you normally throw away should be kept.
- Glass or metal medicine containers;
- Plastic boxes made for sweets, cards, cottons, spices . . .;
- Jamjars, instant coffee jars;
- Mineral water bottles;

A caterpillar of a swallowtail butterfly on almond tree leaves

2. The butterfly net

Good butterfly nets are expensive but you can make your own.

You will need:
    1.40 m (54 in) stiff wire
    0.80 m (30 in) bamboo rod (a piece of old fishing rod).
    A square of old curtain net, 1.10 m × 0.70 m (42 in × 28 in).

    Around a circle of stiff wire you should fix a large pocket of net or fine nylon. The base should be rounded as in the diagram.
    Bind the two ends of the wire tightly with string for a distance of 20 cm (8 in) along the bamboo rod.

circle of stiff wire

the ends of the wire should be
bound tightly round the rod

30 cm

(12 in)

bamboo rod

pocket of fine
net material (curtain net)

60 cm

(24 in)

"There is plenty of room!
My wings won't be damaged."

rounded base

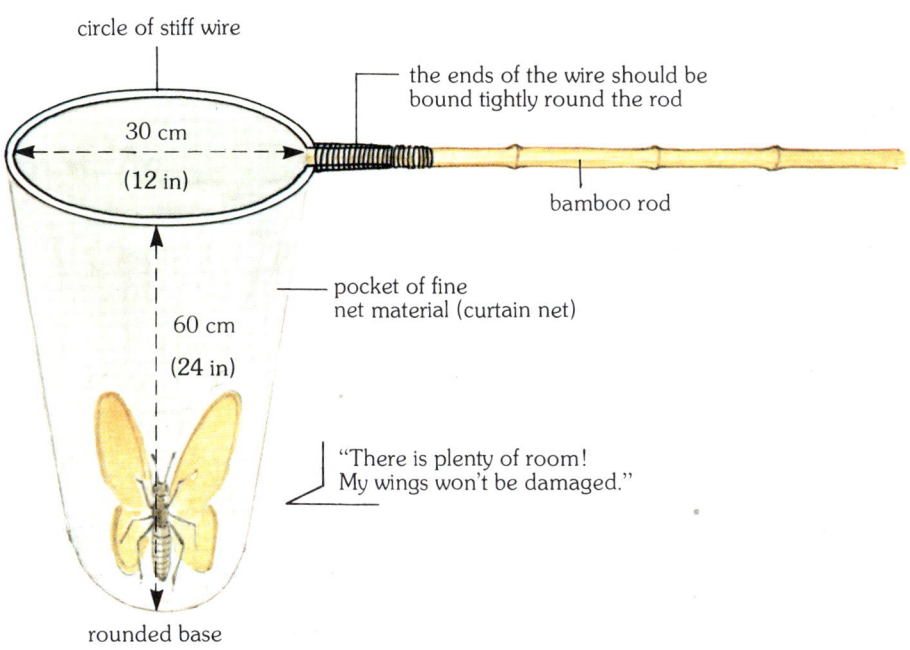

Open the net wide, catch the butterfly, bring the net close to yourself and close it with your hand

Fly and beetle traps

1. Fly-trap

You may need to catch some flies, either to study them or as food for the frogs or lizards which you are keeping.

Here is a very simple arrangement which you can use either as a fly-trap, or a food distributor, if you wish.

To make it you will need:
2 empty mineral water bottles.
A little bran, sand or sawdust.
About 20 cm (8 in) of transparent hose-pipe.
A piece of black paper.

a. Making the trap
Have the two bottles cut as in diagrams A and B. Retain parts 1 and 2 and place part 2, inverted, on part 1. The result should be diagram C.

You should then pierce the side of the bottle at 3 making a hole big enough for your length of hose-pipe. Close it for the time being with adhesive tape.

b. How the trap works
Place a piece of raw fish or meat on the sand or bran at the bottom of the bottle, then place your trap on the window-sill.

The flies will soon be attracted by the meat and enter the trap. Few will escape.

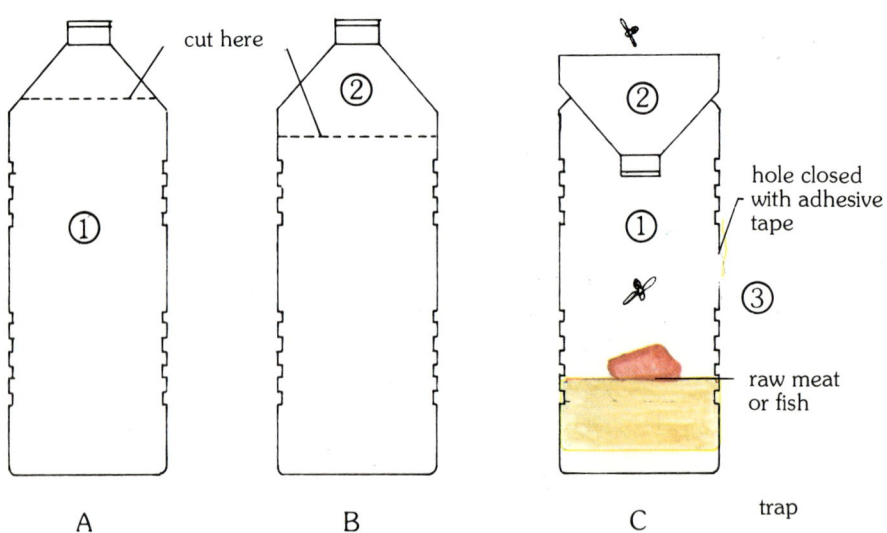

A   B   C   trap

2. Food distributor

When you have caught enough flies in your trap, make a sleeve with the black paper and, using a circle of the same paper, cover part 2. Remove the tape from 3 and insert one end of the pipe into it, putting the other end in the terrarium. The flies will be attracted by the light and move from the bottle to the terrarium.

Very often flies will have laid eggs on the meat and you will have fresh food supplies for your tenants for some time.

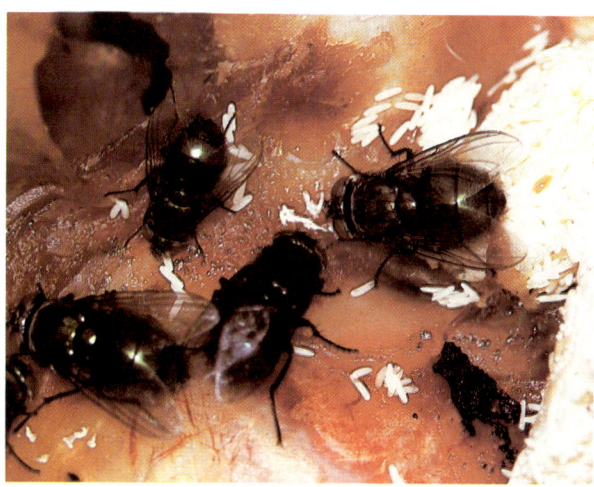

Flies will breed easily in the trap. In about 3 weeks the eggs will hatch into young flies and there will be plenty of food for the inhabitants of your terrarium

3.   A beetle trap

Certain insects feed on the flesh of other animals. You can catch them in the following way:

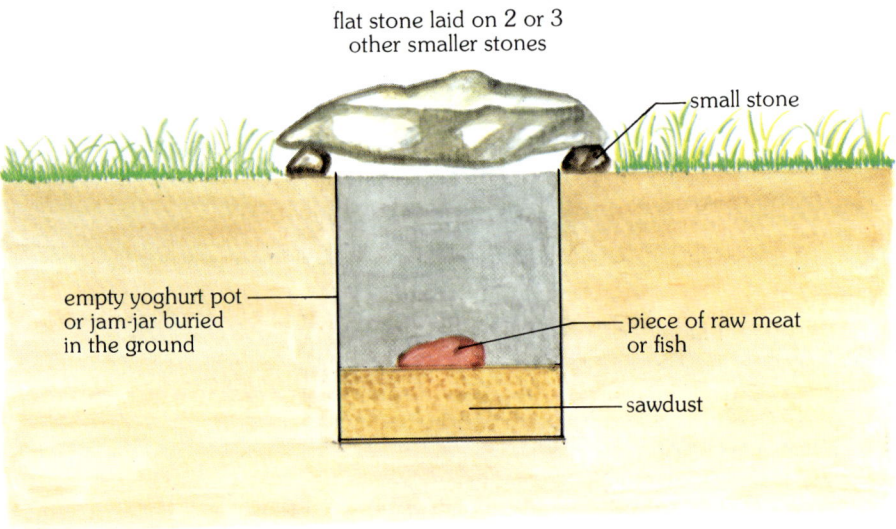

flat stone laid on 2 or 3
other smaller stones

small stone

empty yoghurt pot
or jam-jar buried
in the ground

piece of raw meat
or fish

sawdust

Leave the trap for a short time. The insects attracted by the piece of meat or fish will fall into the pot and won't be able to get out again.

You should remove each insect and place it gently into a terrarium (page 13) where it will feed on small pieces of raw meat.

Installing the insects

1. Field insects

a. How to catch them

You can catch these insects with your hands, but it would be quicker to use a butterfly net. Sweep through the grass, as if you were mowing. After a dozen sweeps you will be surprised to see that you have collected a variety of insects: crickets, mantis, grasshoppers, ladybirds, weevils, bugs, etc.

b. How to install them

You will put your catch, when you return home or to the classroom, in a simple cage (see pages 6 and 7), where you should try to recreate their natural habitat.

Put a little earth at the bottom of the cage, a few dry leaves, some small branches, one or two twigs with leaves on them. Sow some seeds (wheat, maize, sunflower). Spray everything with a little water each day, keep the atmosphere slightly humid.

You have created what we call a "Field Terrarium".

Crickets in a terrarium

2. Insects found in bushes

a. Capture

Place an open umbrella upside down beneath some branches. Using a stick, hit the branches hard. The frightened insects will fall and land in the umbrella. You can catch bugs, ladybirds, weevils, caterpillars, etc.

b. Installation

Put the insects into the "Field Terrarium". (See page 13).

3. Marsh insects

a. How to catch them

You can use your butterfly net or use a makeshift net with a nylon stocking and a wire circle 20 cm (8 in) in diameter (use the instructions on page 9). Drag your net through the water and you will have a good catch: tadpoles, waterboatmen (see photograph below), dragonfly larvae, etc.

b. Installation

An aquarium is needed. Don't forget to put some plants in it. For food, see page 18, but in the meantime you can give them the same food as for goldfish.

4. Butterflies

a. How to catch them

When you see a butterfly, don't rush towards it, as you risk frightening it so that it will fly away out of your reach.

Note its flight pattern and the plants on which it rests. Usually, unless it has been disturbed, it returns to the same spot. You can quickly calculate where it is likely to rest and you must be ready.

Once you have caught it, close the net with your hand. Put a large jar carefully into the net and try to get the butterfly into it, without damaging the insect. You shouldn't keep it in the jar for too long.

A six spot Burnet moth

b. Installation

As soon as you reach your home or the school put your butterfly into the simple cage, (see pages 6 and 7) with a bunch of flowers. Note its proboscis.

The Common Blue butterfly

The Brimstone butterfly

5. Caterpillars

a. How to catch them

When you are out walking, you will often have the chance to find caterpillars. If you want to study them properly, pick them up very carefully, as they are very delicate.

Never pick up a furry caterpillar with your naked hand, as some of them can produce a rash.

Always pick a few branches from the plant where you find the caterpillar. It is very probable that the plant provides its food. If a large caterpillar does not eat, don't get worried. It is on the point of turning into a chrysalis.

Caterpillar of one of the family Vanessidae

Caterpillar of the family Noctuidae

Spurge hawk moth caterpillar

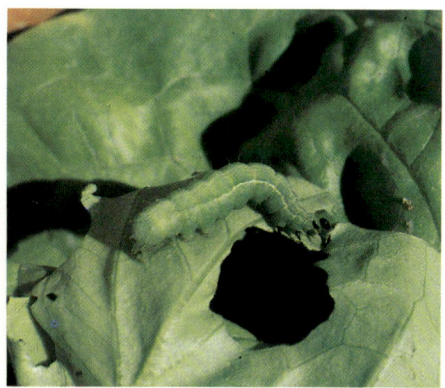

A caterpillar on a lettuce

b. Installation

1. If you have a small aquarium, put it upright on one of its small sides. Put some branches in a jar of water inside the aquarium. Caterpillars will live on these branches and feed on the leaves. To prevent the caterpillars drowning, put a pierced cork in the mouth of the jar. A piece of fine mesh wire-netting or net will prevent the butterflies from escaping.

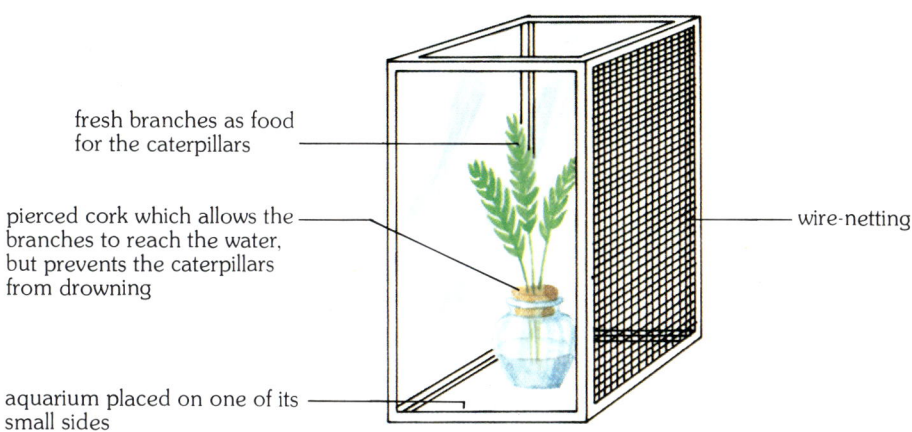

fresh branches as food for the caterpillars

pierced cork which allows the branches to reach the water, but prevents the caterpillars from drowning

aquarium placed on one of its small sides

wire-netting

2. If you don't have an aquarium, here is a simple piece of equipment which will allow you to study the caterpillars.

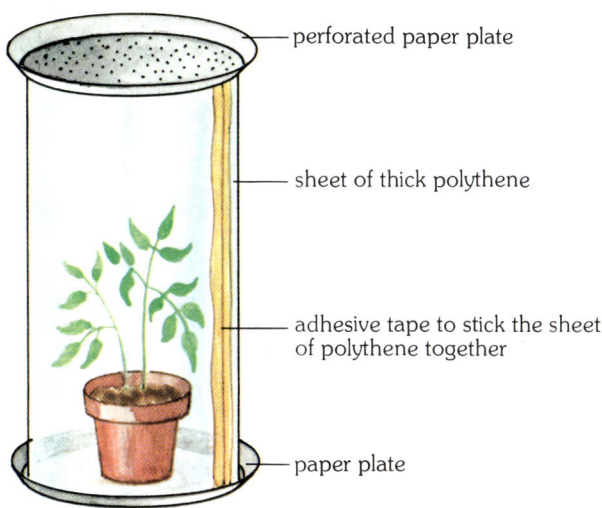

perforated paper plate

sheet of thick polythene

adhesive tape to stick the sheet of polythene together

paper plate

Always take care to remove old branches and give the caterpillars fresh leaves to eat.

Name of Insect	Season	Special Conditions	Food	Predators
ROSE-CHAFER larva (white grub) adult	all the year in humus March to October	leaf-mould some flowers (lilac, rose)	vegetable moulds, nectar, ripe fruit	beetles, moles, toads, slow-worms, birds
LADYBIRD	March to October	put a germinating potato in the terrarium (aphids will breed on it)	aphids	birds
CRICKET	April to October	box with damp sand for laying eggs	cereal, seedlings, lettuce	mantis, adders
CATERPILLAR	March to October	see pages 16 and 17	nutritious plants on which caterpillars feed	birds, millipedes, certain hymenoptera
DRAGONFLY	all the year	aquarium with some branches emerging from the water	tadpoles, worms, larvae water-snails, tiny fish	carnivorous fish, frogs, birds
MANTIS	June to Sept. – Oct.	look for adults and eggs in Autumn	crickets, insects	birds, ants
BLOW-FLY	March to October	see page 10 for capture	pieces of meat	lizards, spiders, birds, toads
WATER-BOATMAN	all the year	aquarium	tadpoles, worms, larvae, tiny fish	aquatic birds
BUTTERFLY	March to Sept.–Oct.	a bunch of flowers, water with sugar	flower nectar sugared water	birds, frogs
BUGS	March to October	field terrarium with plants	umbelliferous plants and vegetables	birds, toads
PYRRHOCORUS	March to October	bark and dead leaves	dead leaves, dandelions	birds, slow-worms, lizards
GRASSHOPPER	April to October	box with damp sand for laying eggs	grass, seeds, small insects	praying mantis, birds, lizards, slow-worms
COLEOPTERA (larva = "mealworm")	all the year at shops selling fishing tackle	box with bran, flour, bread and a damp sponge	bran, flour, bread	the larva is eaten by lizards, slow-worms and water-tortoise

Mealworms well installed

A mealworm (× 2)

A garden rose-chafer

A dragonfly nymph

A grasshopper

Pyrrhocorus, firebug

The ant-hill

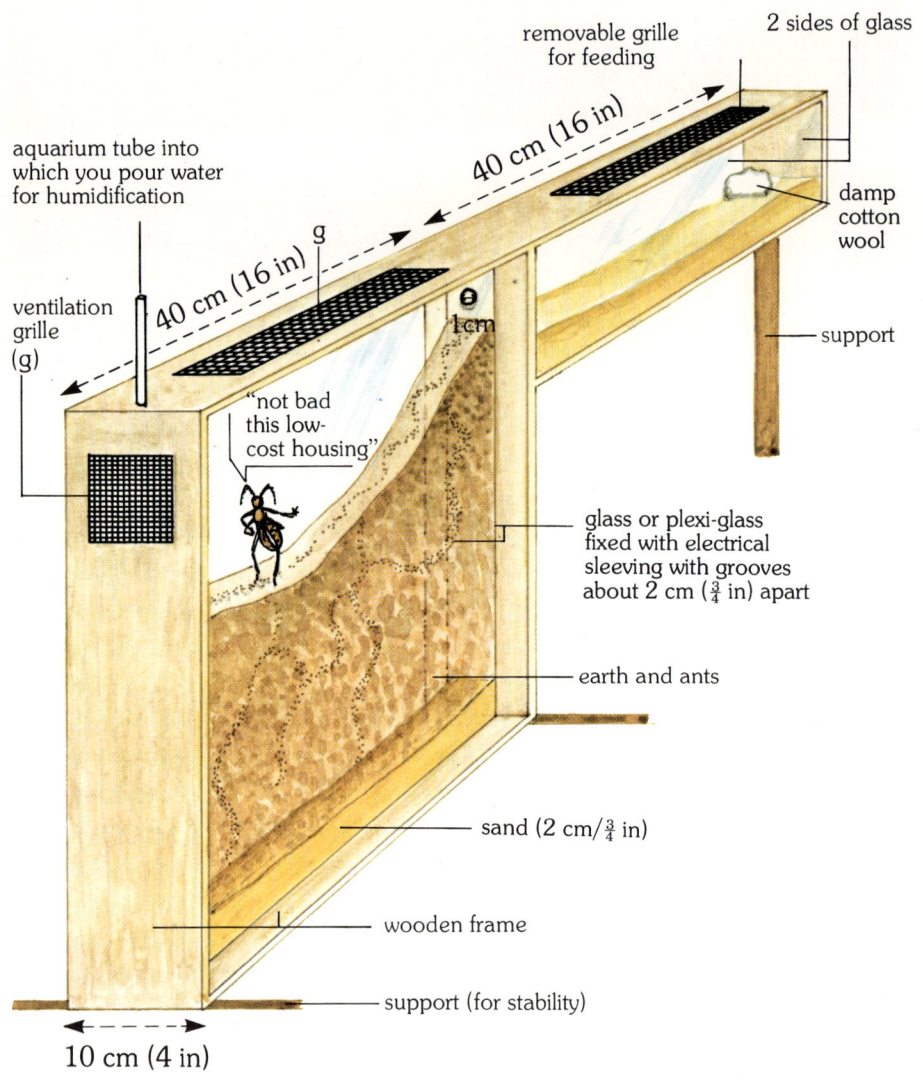

removable grille
for feeding

2 sides of glass

40 cm (16 in)

aquarium tube into
which you pour water
for humidification

damp
cotton
wool

ventilation
grille
(g)

40 cm (16 in) g

1 cm

support

"not bad
this low-
cost housing"

glass or plexi-glass
fixed with electrical
sleeving with grooves
about 2 cm ($\frac{3}{4}$ in) apart

earth and ants

sand (2 cm/$\frac{3}{4}$ in)

wooden frame

support (for stability)

10 cm (4 in)

a. Collecting ants

When you see an anthill in its natural state, try with a shovel to collect as
many insects as possible and bring them back to your artificial ant-hill in a
sealed bucket.

b. Installation

Put the entire contents of the bucket into the artificial ant-hill. The ants will
reorganize their society, if you have been lucky enough to bring back a queen.
    You should feed the ants on sugar, seeds, insects and meat.

Spiders

a. How to catch them
You can catch them by hand in the fields, with your butterfly net or with the technique of the upturned umbrella (see page 14).

b. Installation
You can use a simple cage (see pages 6 and 7). Put in some twigs and some damp earth.

To feed your spiders you will need live insects. You can use your fly distributor described on page 11.

Animals from a humid habitat

a. How to catch them

You will find, under stones, on damp tree stumps, or in the ground, many small animals which we often pass unnoticed: millipedes (polydesmus, geophilus), woodlice, earthworms, may-bugs, grubs, slugs, snails, slow-worms, etc. Collect them in a large box with some earth and decomposing leaves which will provide them with food.

b. Installation

You can install the animal, depending on its size:

1. In a simple cage (see pages 6 and 7) taking care to cover the top with glass or plastic to prevent the interior from drying out.

2. In the large terrarium (page 24) which is very suitable for this type of animal population.

3. In a pot with a water reserve that you can make as follows:

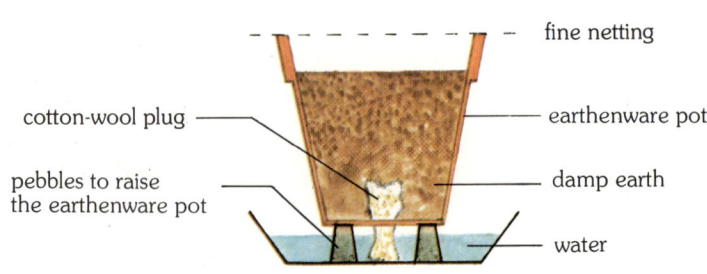

cotton-wool plug — fine netting

pebbles to raise the earthenware pot — earthenware pot — damp earth — water

A slow-worm

An earth-worm

A slug

Millipedes

A large terrarium

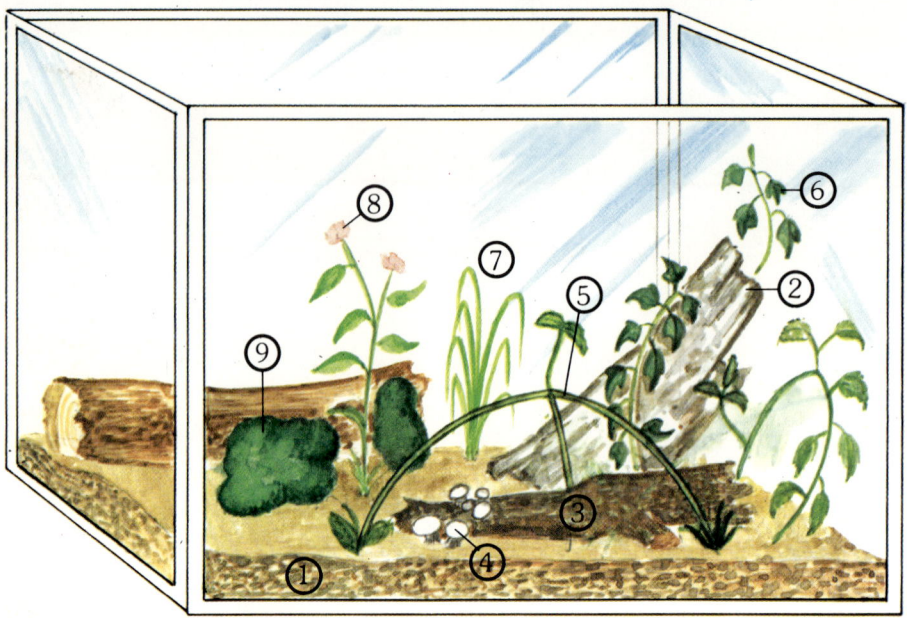

1. Earth + humus + bits of wood, bark, etc.
2. Bark with insect larvae.
3. Dead wood, pieces of tree stumps.
4. Young fungi.
5. Brambles, with one layered naturally.
6. Growing ivy.
7. Grasses.
8. Flowering plants such as daisies.
9. Moss.

This terrarium will allow you to study, either at home or in school, "a fragment of nature" and observe the intense activity in each element of this natural world in miniature.

You will need a large aquarium, 80 cm (32 in) in length, in which you place the following items from the woods or roadside verges making sure first that you have permission to do so:

Use a spade to gather some humus with a little earth. Uproot some ferns, ivy and very young seedlings. Collect a few acorns, chestnuts or other seeds from trees, some dead wood, bark, bits of old tree-stumps, etc.

First put a layer of earth in the aquarium in which you will place a selection of plants. Next add the humus, pieces of tree-stump and dead wood, leaves, seeds (acorns, chestnuts), and tufts of moss.

Spray everything with a little water as earth is always damp in the woods, and cover the top of the terrarium with a sheet of glass or plastic.

You should place the terrarium away from direct sunlight, so as to imitate the light filtering through the woods.

This terrarium will need no further maintenance, as a natural cycle will develop. You will be surprised to see fauna appear which you had not noticed, in particular the animals from a humid habitat described on page 22, as well as new plants and fungi. You will notice the slow decomposition of the dead leaves and the intense activity of the insects.

The terrarium can be kept throughout the school year. Once you have no further use for it, you should replant the flowers, etc. where you found them.

1

2

3

1. Black beetles.
2. A chestnut germinating.
3. Insect larvae on a dead tree-stump.

Freshwater aquariums

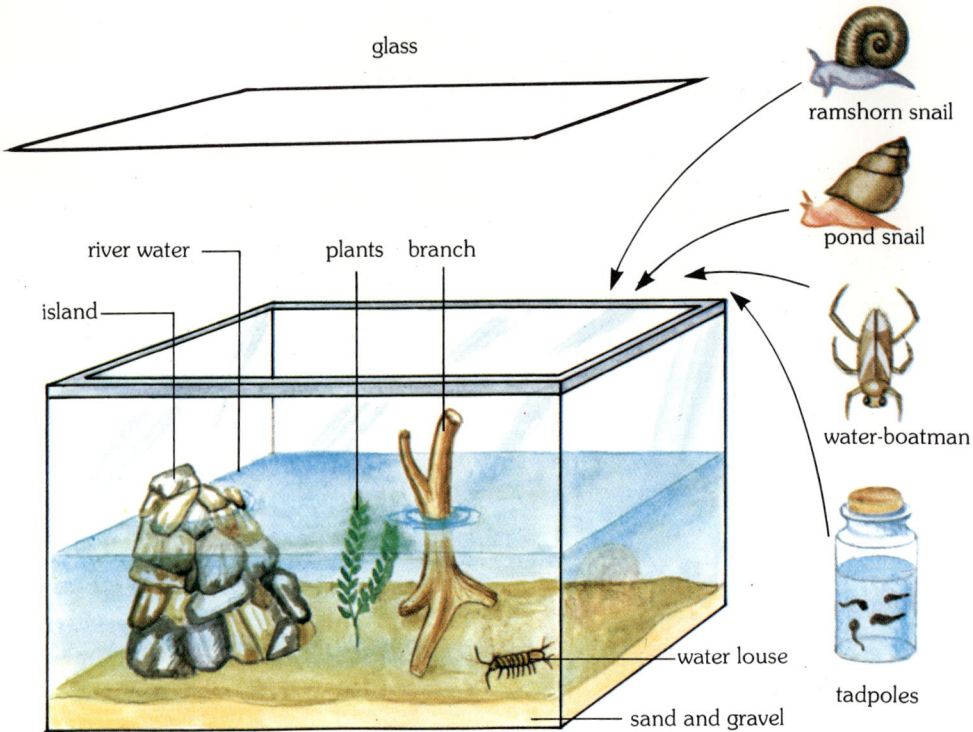

It is interesting to have an aquarium about 80 cm (32 in) in length with a glass cover to it. This will prevent the animals from jumping out of the aquarium, protect the water from dust and cut down on the evaporation of water.

a. Installation

Put some sand at the bottom in which you plant some freshwater plants. You can also include an aerator with a pump.

b. Inhabitants

Fish

Aquatic fauna from marshes and pools: tadpoles, leeches, water-boatmen and all sorts of larvae, etc.

Paludariums for frogs and toads

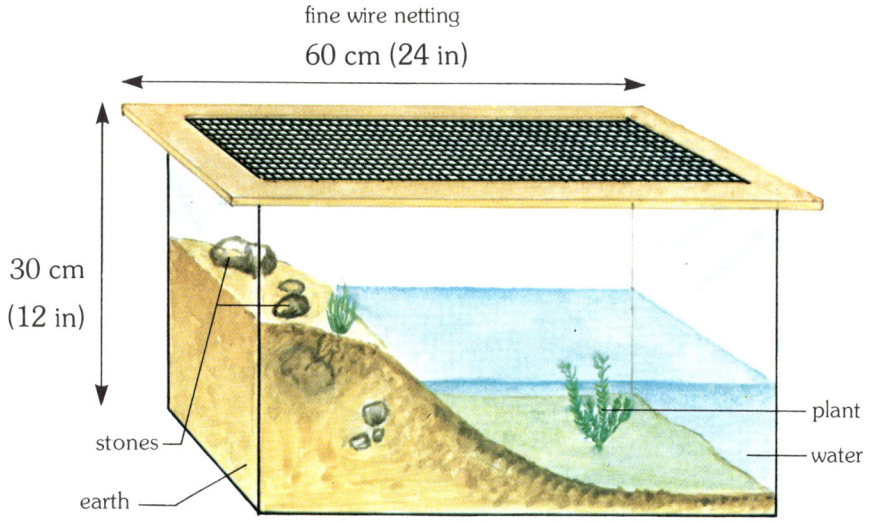

fine wire netting

60 cm (24 in)

30 cm
(12 in)

stones

earth

plant

water

Create a slope in the aquarium, using earth, from a height of 20 cm (8 in) to 5 cm (2 in). Put in a few stones and water-loving plants. Pour in carefully about 10 cm (4 in) of water. A part of the slope must be above water.

Cover with netting to prevent the frogs escaping. Install the food distributor (see page 11).

Two fire salamanders, damp moss, a water receptacle and food (maggots and pupae, which become flies) in a terrarium

Terrariums for reptiles

1.   Dry terrarium

In this you can put lizards, slow-worms, etc.

Installation

In an aquarium or a simple cage place a layer of earth, sand, and bark in equal proportions, a water receptacle at ground level, a few flat stones and a green plant (a fern for example).

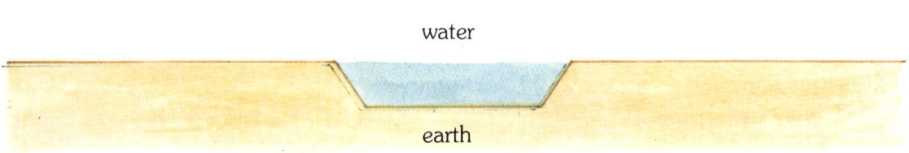

water

earth

   Now you can put in the inhabitants.
Don't forget to give them live insects: crickets, flies (see distributor on page 11), spiders, butterflies, caterpillars, earthworms, and mealworms.

2.   Humid terrarium

See instructions on page 22 or page 24.

Cages for hamsters or mice

You can buy very pretty little cages for hamsters or mice. You are sure to be able to make some interesting studies of a hamster in this sort of cage, but both the hamster and the mouse love to burrow. We therefore suggest that you put them in the cage we have designed below. They will build their own home in a great hurry!

House mouse

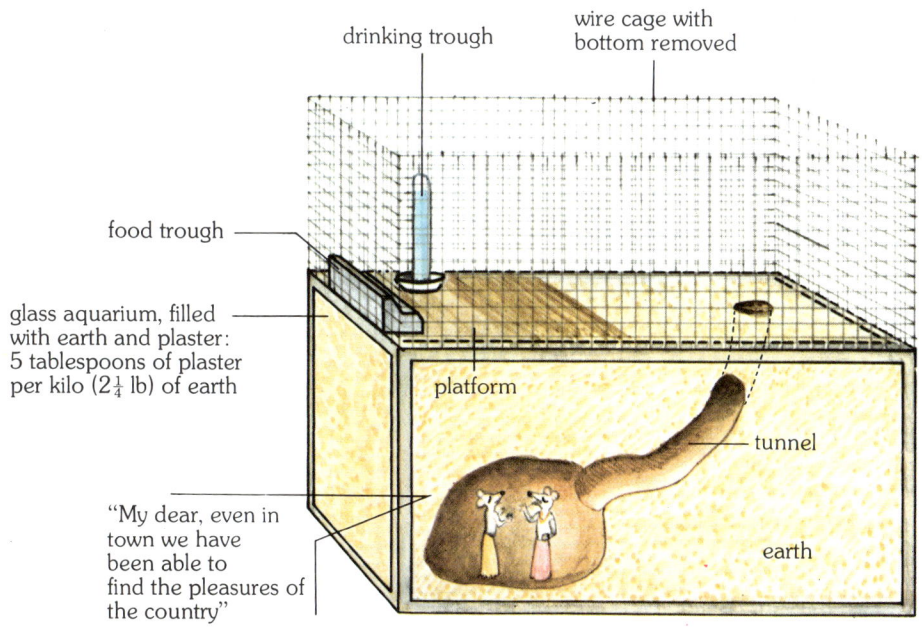

drinking trough

wire cage with bottom removed

food trough

glass aquarium, filled with earth and plaster: 5 tablespoons of plaster per kilo (2¼ lb) of earth

platform

tunnel

earth

"My dear, even in town we have been able to find the pleasures of the country"

Aquarium: A tank designed to hold water to keep alive animals from an aquatic habitat: fish, water-boatmen, dragonfly larvae, etc.

Carnivore: An animal which feeds on other living animals.

Chrysalis: Third stage in the development of butterflies. The chrysalis sometimes hangs from plants on silk threads or is buried in the ground. Some of them are wrapped in a silk cocoon.

Function: The particular role of an organ or equipment. The proboscis of a butterfly sucks the nectar from a flower; sucking is its function.

Hymenoptera: Ants, wasps and bees, and similar insects.

Habitat: The natural environment in which an animal lives, including the place and its conditions (light, temperature, humidity, etc.). A marsh or a pile of leaves both constitute a habitat.

Life cycle: This includes all the developmental stages of a living being from one generation to the next.

Nutritious Plant: A plant on which certain insects (caterpillars, bugs, etc.), feed.

Organ: A part of the body which has a clearly defined function: e.g. a wing enables a bird to fly.

Paludarium: A tank equipped for animals living in water and on land (terrapin, triton, salamander, frog, tadpole).

Predator: An animal which feeds on other living animals.

Terrarium: An artificial home for land animals (crickets, grasshoppers, etc.).

INDEX